Girl, Adjust Your Crown, A 31 Day Women's Devotional

By Carol D. Jackson

FOREWARD

I dedicate this women's devotional to my mother; Vera Johnson Rensch. We affectionately call her, "Sweet Vee". I'd like to thank her for loving me and my siblings. Thank you for nurturing us, and for praying fervently and definitely without ceasing for her children. For always ensuring my siblings and myself stayed out of harm's way. She cared for us so eloquently and adequately; I can honestly say, "there's nothing comparable to a "mother's love". We had everything we needed, and Moma even gave us some of the things we wanted. Everyone said we were spoiled and rotten, no we were LOVED. Moma taught us that having Jesus as our Personal Lord and Savior is the only way to live. Thank you to My dear sweet

mother for ALL the love, guidance and
CONFIDENCE that

you've ALWAYS spoken over my life, I
absolutely ADORE YOU Moma.
♥ ♥ ♥

Day 1

Life's Challenges

1 Peter 5:7 (KJV) Casting all your care upon him; for he careth for you.

We've all experienced things not going the way we'd hoped. Many of us have found ourselves disappointed because of "failed plans". No matter where we are in our walk with Christ; We all have feelings and emotions and we want things to work in our favor. Sometimes, things

just don't turn out the way we expected.
Trust God, and use every "failed"

opportunity to praise Him in the process.
Life is full of challenges. We'll

experience them, day in and day out.
Perhaps today you woke up to your car
not starting . This. After having decided
last month that you no longer needed to
renew your car assistance membership
because you hadn't used it in over two
years. You've got a meeting at the office;
that has been on the calendar since last
year and it's mandatory. Not to mention
your toddler woke up cranky! He has a
high fever, and now you've got to call off
of work. Or You've been watching your
calories lately and you've shed some
pounds, so you wanted to treat yourself to
something; The other day, you went to

your favorite bakery to get your favorite banana pudding cupcake But! the person ahead of you just bought the last one. Or

even worse, your father's health has been great, up until last week. Now, he's scheduled for open heart surgery in a few days. What's next? You're now feeling depleted, defeated and worn. You're so unsure of what is going on and why! You know God has a unique way of making plans and decisions on our behalf; after all he created you. Instead of giving in and giving the enemy place... WORSHIP The Lord in the midst of your circumstances whether good or bad. Thank God for what He has yet done in your life. You are not defeated, you're an Overcomer. You are a Conqueror! When the enemy weighs in and tries to burden you, cast all your cares on God! Praise your way through all adversity. God is Amazing. He's Loving and He's able to see you, love you and heal you right where you are.

Prayer: Lord Jesus, forgive me for being doubtful and falling prey to fear. I pray that you will continue to carry me, to encourage me and guide me in this life even when I don't understand my circumstances. Help me Lord Jesus to pray without ceasing, no matter what it is I'm going through. I thank you for doing it, In Jesus name. ~Amen.

Day 2

God Loves You! Flaws And All

John 3:16 For God so loved the world, that He gave His only begotten Son that whosoever believeth in Him shall not perish but have everlasting life.

Dealing with depression is never easy. I can speak on this subject as I had suffered with it for many years. Until I decided I had a choice to be free and happy. Depression is a spirit, and an ungodly one. It comes to rob you of your

joy, your peace and your quality of life.
God loves you. He loves you when you
think you're a nobody. He loves you

when you sin. Yet His hope for you is
eternal life. God's love for you always
remains. Depression is exhausting. Be
not discouraged, for God loves you.
Even when you choose not to love
yourself or when you don't give yourself
grace. Jesus has genuine love for every
person individually. The sacrifice he
made on Calvary proves it. He was
ridiculed, beaten, stripped of all dignity,
spit upon, degraded, devalued and
eventually murdered all because of His
love for you.

 Why continue to question your self-
worth? Why beat yourself up based on
what the enemy says? Bind and rebuke
him in Jesus name. Surrender your life

completely to Jesus. He can give you a life of true love, acceptance and understanding. You'll never again

feel lonely. You will begin to live and operate in the purpose He predestined for your life. Depression is torment. It's only purpose is to destroy you. To keep you bound, gripped with sadness, to confuse you. The enemies play is to disrupt the purpose God has for you. Jesus said I come that you might have life and have it more abundantly. Confess your sins, receive new life through Jesus. Affirm great things over your life, speak life over yourself. Encourage yourself in The Lord!!! Love on you and all aspects of who you are, you're ROYALTY, Jesus doesn't create garbage!!!

Prayer: Help me Dear Lord to forgive myself as you have forgiven me through

my confession of sin. Teach me Lord to
recognize my worth, despite my mistakes
and past failures.   Show me Lord Jesus

to live in the present, through your
constant presence. When I'm fearful,
confused and experiencing the feeling of
becoming overwhelmed; Lead me to call
upon your name Lord. Teach me to trust

you, to praise and worship you through
everything. Teach me to walk in your
grace, your love, and all the good that
you have afforded me. Thank you Lord
for the greatest gift; The gift of your love
and forgiveness. ~Amen.

Day 3

Feel Unworthy?

Psalm 149:4 For God taketh pleasure in his people.

Have you ever had one of those days where you felt inadequate? Unworthy? Broken, used and abused? The pain so deep that you felt there was no way out. The truth is that we all have. There is liberty and grace in knowing who we are and in who created us. We will face many challenges, even trials where people won't like you, some won't accept

you. They'll despise your suggestions
and carry a strong dislike for perhaps

your taste in shoes. They won't care for
your recipes and oh, the way you apply

your makeup is beyond dreadful
according to them. That's their thoughts
and opinions. The scripture Psalm 149:4
states that God takes pleasure in his
people, God is aware of all your flaws,
and your indifferences. Yet, He loves
you so much. If we would adopt the
unfailing love that God has for us we'd
lead a more productive and happy life.

Instead of allowing others to dictate
who you are or what you should be,
Thank God for his creation of you! God

designed YOU with purpose. God's purpose over your life has nothing to do with what someone thought or even

thinks you should be. Change your way of thinking. Continue to pray and trust God to deliver you from the burden of trying to always satisfy others; Stop

being a people pleaser at any cost. Put your hope to work in pleasing The Father. After all, He created you and everything He made is good. When you feel you bring nothing extra to the table. When others convey to you, you're worthless, remember that The One and Only True Living God takes complete pleasure in His creation of you and your uniqueness.

Prayer: Lord Jesus deliver me from people. Teach me Lord to trust you when I'm hurting. Especially when I'm feeling inadequate and troubled. Help me to not allow others to tell me who I am or who I

should be. Silence their negative opinions of me in my head. Lord, I want to be grateful for my life. Teach me to love myself, thereby being able to love others. Even when I don't agree with the thoughts of others. Show me how to

respect them. Help me to be an obedient daughter. Help me to be an heiress to your kingdom with whom you are well pleased. ~Amen

Day 4

Choosing To Forgive Others

Ephesians 4:31-32

Let all bitterness, and wrath, and anger, and clamour, and evil speaking, be put away from you, with all malice:

And be ye kind one to another, tenderhearted, forgiving one another, even as God for Christ's sake hath forgiven you.

Who has wronged you recently? Who broke your heart? Who didn't come through with what they promised?

Whoever it was deserves your forgiveness. None of us are perfect;

Jesus Christ is the only one perfected. Don't continue to cut your blessings short by holding unnecessary "grudges". The Bible tells us that Jesus came, that we might have life, and live more abundantly. How is it that we as forgiven human beings can't forgive one another? We must STOP operating in foolishness. Unforgiveness and carrying grudges is time wasted. Ponder on all the work you can be doing for The Lord, yet you choose to be mad. You may say : "I'm

not mad, I just don't deal with them".
Imagine how lost we'd all be if The Lord
just stopped communicating with us for
what we've done. There would be no
salvation, no repentance. We'd be

forever lost. Forgive yourself first for
sinning and then forgive the person,
because God honors that. We can't walk
around preaching and praising with

stained hearts. It won't work and The
Lord isn't pleased. How can you expect
God to forgive you? When you REFUSE
to forgive another? Pray to The Lord
about carrying unnecessary weight and
forgive so you can be blessed.

Prayer: Father, forgive me for my
foolishness. Help me to continually walk
in love. Help me to understand that we

aren't perfect; we're just forgiven. When I stand before you Father, it's my desire to be pleasing in thy site. Harboring malice isn't your will, nor is it your way. Help me Lord Jesus to operate in the

manner in which you spoke all throughout the Bible. Teach me to forgive and operate in love. Forgive me for carrying unforgiveness in my heart and help me to handle situations such as this, differently the next time. ~ Amen.

Day 5

We Serve A Multi-Faceted God

Psalm 46:10 Be still, and know that I am
God: I will be exalted among the
heathen, I will be exalted in all the earth.

Hey Sis, I want to remind you of How
good our GOD truly is. No one can
compare. When I think of God's
unfailing power and love; I'm also
reminded of how He's able to see things,
all circumstances and situations before
us. As He goes before us, He's enforcing

and commanding protection over our lives. God is a gem. Gleaming, glistening and bright. He's omnipresent, always here in our midst. He's all

knowing, and absolutely NOTHING is difficult for Him. For with Him all things
are possible. God is Self-Existent, Eternal, Pure, Transcendent Self-sufficient, and Aesity. He's omnipotent and immutable. He's God all by Himself.

Prayer: Father, help me your daughter, to refrain from trying to handle and juggle everything on my own. Help me to acknowledge your love and admiration for me, as your daughter, a descendant of royalty. Keep my heart open to receive your guidance through discernment, fasting and praying. Keep me on the path of righteousness as you said you'd lead me. ~Amen

Day 6

Fear, Are You Bound By It?
Psalm 23:4 Yea, though I walk through the valley of the shadow of death, I will fear no evil. For thou art with me; thy rod and thy staff they comfort me.

Fear can literally come upon us at the most unexpected of times. Being careful of what we partake in, in this world is essential to guarding our hearts and minds. As daughters of The King, we are taught not to walk nor operate in the spirit of fear. When fear attempts to consume you, you must first go to God in prayer. Binding and rebuking the enemy, as he has no authority over you! We can

always find hope in Jesus as He is our anchor in any storm, that life tries to throw at us. I came up with an acronym for FEAR.

My hope is that you'll use this when fear tears it's ugly head. It's also a great affirmation:
I'm choosing to handle fear by:
Facing
Everything
Amazingly
Remarkably

God wants us to walk in the fullness that only HE can provide. Change your thoughts on fear and walk in the blessings that are so freely yours.

Prayer: Lord, forgive me when I become fearful as I know you are always with me. Your word declares you would never leave nor forsake me. Help me Lord to be mindful of things that may inflict fear within me. Teach me to be wise in all of my life choices. Continue to show me your will and your way asI know that I can never go wrong when following your lead. In Jesus name I pray. ~Amen

Day 7

Let Go & Let God

Phillipians 4:6-7 KJV Be careful for
nothing; but in everything by prayer and
supplication with Thanksgiving, let your
requests be made known unto God. And
the peace of God, which passeth all
understanding, shall keep your hearts and
minds through Christ Jesus.

Stop! Don't worry any longer about what
it is you can't fix. Sis, the battle isn't
yours; it's the Lord's . God is a

gentleman and He will kindly step out of your way, should you feel you don't need His help. He said he'd give us the very desires of our heart. Look no longer at

the timing of things, where you are financially or anything else that causes you unnecessary stress. The Lord promised us in The Word of God that He'd freely give unto us. Give God the glory, praise Him in advance for the things you've requested. His timing or His ways are unlike ours. Yet, His timing is always perfect. Oftentimes, we're focused on the wait; we feel God is taking too long. Seeing things from that perspective will cause you to feel the WEIGHT of the WAIT. Trust God, He is merciful. He'll deliver, but on and in His timing . Give God your every weight; He will strengthen you.

Prayer: Father forgive me for trying to handle and juggle things on my own. I

need your guidance. I patiently await your new work, in me. As I walk by faith, I will trust your lead. I thank you for loving me, I thank you for providing me with everything I need. Thank you for being Jehovah Jireh, The God who provides. I love you Father. ~ Amen.

Day 8

Repentance

1 John 1:9 KJV If we confess our sins, he
is faithful and just to forgive us our sins,
and to cleanse us from all
unrighteousness.

Tired of living the raggedy life that
produces nothing but hurt? Full of
confusion and tired of feeling
incomplete? Are you looking for peace
and assurance? Are you tired of fighting

with the devil? Are you ready to live a life where everything isn't perfect, but there is a promise of eternal life and greater days to come? Lastly, are you just ready to repent? If so, let's do this. Let's

pray the prayer of repentance so you can begin to live a life more abundantly.

Prayer: Heavenly Father forgive me for my sins; I come to you, confessing my sin and Lord I ask your forgiveness. I'm here acknowledging what I have done. I'm confessing my sin unto you today. Please forgive me Lord? Today I choose to turn away from sin. Please forgive me for those I've hurt, and Lord I ask you to have them to also forgive me. I desire from this moment forward, to seek to restore my wrongs done to others. I pray daily that you would help me to stay on the right path. I will read my bible and pray daily, asking you to strengthen me. I ask you to give me knowledge and understanding of The Holy Bible as I

begin to read it and apply to my life. ~ Amen.

Day 9

What Is LOVE?

John 13:35 KJV By this shall all men
know ye are my disciples, if ye have love
one to another.

Love is patient, love is kind. It doesn't
envy, it does not boast, it is not proud. It
does not dishonor others, it's not self-
seeking, it's not easily angered and it
keeps no records of wrongs. Love
doesn't delight in evil, yet it rejoices in

the truth. The love God speaks of in this passage of scripture is what is known as the "agape" kind of love. This "agape" kind of love, refers to God's divine love.

God requires us to love everyone. Love protects, it always trusts, it secures, it offers hope and preservation. The "agape" love doesn't come with stipulations, there are absolutely no strings attached. God wants us to love without recompense. He wants us literally to love the hell out of people. This God kind of love can only happen with persistent reading of the scriptures and praying fervently that God would instill His likeness and His beautiful attributes in all of His children.

Prayer : Father, I come to you in The Name Of Jesus, I request your mercy. Lord, I repent of anything that displeases you. I ask that you would clean me up. Allow me to see others with the eyes of love as you see me. Help me Lord to love, to love genuinely. To love people as you, Jesus Christ loves the church.

Fill me up with your AGAPE love.
~Amen

Day 10

God Is With You

Psalms 46:1 KJV
God is our refuge and strength, a very
present help in trouble.

Despite your journey. This sometimes
vicious, challenging, hurtful and
inconsistent life can be hard to swallow.
However; through it all, God has been
with you. God's desire is to love you, to
protect you through the ups and downs in

life. God was there when you lost your job. He was there when your car was repoed. God was there when you experienced that painful breakup, that

you felt you'd never heal from. The Father had been with you all along. He has and will NEVER leave you. Do yourself a favor, start today by focusing on and in the positive. God Is ALWAYS there to lift you up. He's always around to comfort and encourage you. He is always a call or prayer away. Call on Him, all you have to do is say "Abba Father". He will heal you, He will deliver you and HE will most definitely set you free all you have to do is ask. It's free. Just ask Him for what it is you need.

Prayer: Lord Jesus, I come to you humbly asking for your help. I know I haven't made the best decisions in my life. Please forgive me for neglecting to acknowledge your beautiful presence. I need you to help me to make better decisions concerning my life. From this day forward I will not only say I know you, I will live my life according to what you say is Christlike. I realize that I need you in all aspects of my life, I know I can do nothing without you. Thank you Jesus for all that you've done in my life. Every danger unseen and I thank you for your hedge of protection over myself and my family members. In Jesus name. ~Amen

Day 11

Patiently Waiting On God

Psalms 27:1 KJV

The Lord is my light and my salvation; whom shall I fear? the Lord is the strength of my life; of whom shall I be afraid?

Wait, my Sister on The Lord and be of good courage. Our Heavenly Father has the ability to move mountains and to change and fix ANY situation or circumstance you may be currently experiencing. You may have bills due, wondering how you're going to pay them. But God always has a plan.

Oftentimes, part of The Lord's plan is him allowing us to grow through these situations to increase our faith. Every single thing The Lord has for us is purpose driven. We serve a common sense God. Everything He allows builds character, strength and renewed faith within us. Being a "believer" is a faith walk, God is working in us while we patiently wait on Him.

Prayer: Heavenly Father, I come to you humbly Thanking You for who you are. Thank you for always allowing me to learn a very valuable lesson while I wait. You are Great and Greatly to be praised

and I honor you. Thank you for allowing
my faith to be strengthened during the
times when you are refining me. I could
never tell you how grateful I am for all

the many blessings you have afforded
me. Again I say Thank You Jesus. ~
Amen

Day 12

Let's Chat About FAITH!

Hebrews 11:1 KJV Now faith is the substance of things hoped for, the evidence of things unseen.

You've been on your job for sometime; 5 years and you thought of yourself as an ideal employee. You've been chosen often to do presentations. Lately, you've gone unnoticed. Previously; you and your co-workers worked alongside each other, you complimented one another. You all

worked together in unity. At that time
you truly loved your job. You'd arrive
early to chat with co-workers before your
day started, now things have changed.

You're unhappy because you don't know
where you stand with your manager.
Your co-workers have changed and being
in everyone's presence now has you
feeling uneasy. You've prayed with no
answer in sight from God about direction,
you constantly ask God, should you stay
or should you go? You know the word of
God, God said he'd give you your heart's
desire. You've questioned God, are you
hearing me? Why am I suffering?
Oftentimes, God has to allow us to feel
pressure before a breakthrough. Though
it feels horrible. You feel like you're
now in this "dry" season. God doesn't
seem to be listening. You're still

believing that God can and will change your situation. Sometimes, we choose to move ahead of God. Then it feels that we are worse off than before. Continue to

Trust God in the process, continue to pray and have faith. Don't look at the status of the situation, rest completely in faith, believing by faith that Jesus will change your situation.

Prayer: Lord Jesus please be my fence. Allow me to trust you, even when my situations look hopeless. Show me how to love and press on even in uncomfortable situations. Lord, I know that you said that you'd never leave nor forsake me. Keep me Father from reacting solely on how I feel. Help me Jesus to trust your promises and to refrain from leaning on my own understanding.

Please Lord keep me hopefully as well as prayerful in everything I do. ~Amen

Day 13

Loneliness

Joshua 1:9 Have I not commanded thee? Be strong and of a good courage; be not afraid, neither be thou dismayed: for the LORD thy God is with thee whithersoever thou goest.

Oftentimes we're consumed with the feeling of loneliness. It doesn't matter whether we're married, have children, whether we are in a relationship or even if we're around friends often. The spirit of loneliness can hit anyone, at any time. This is the enemy trying to deceive you. With God you are never alone. The Lord will allow you at times to be by yourself.

However; He's always present.
Sometimes God can only minister to you when you are alone, so He will politely remove people from around you. God loves you and He wants the very best for you.

Be strong Sis, if you are in a season of being alone; seek the Lord and ask Him what is His purpose in your being by yourself so often. He will surely answer. God uses those lonely times to speak to us, sometimes there's correction and other times He wants to coach you into performing an assigned task. God never leaves you, nor will He ever forsake you.

Prayer: Lord help me to understand why I sometimes need to be alone. Help me Father to recognize when you're at work

in me. Help me to not try to fight your processes because I know I will never win. Allow me to be obedient when you are refining me. And allow me to understand that you are in control, that your ways and your thoughts are unlike mine. ~Amen

Day 14

Gracefully Broken

John 14:27 KJV Peace I leave with you,
my peace I give unto you. Let not your
heart be troubled, neither let it be afraid.

As I sat down to write this devotional, I
asked God what does it mean to be
"gracefully broken"?

Being gracefully broken means you're
healing from the situations of your past.
Though you remember them, you know
God is your confidant, He's your help.
You know that you're never alone in

anything because God is always near.
He's here to assure you that everything
you partake in will be blessed because of
your surrendering of your life in being
obedient unto Him. You are assured in
knowing that your past doesn't define
who you are today. Because the Holy
Bible tells you that through repentance all
things have become new.

Being broken gracefully is realizing that
the goal that wasn't accomplished when
you thought it should have been is
coming into fruition. It's about believing

every word and every thought God has spoken over you; He said you are fearfully and wonderfully made. Therefore, your goals are reachable. Being gracefully broken doesn't mean you're perfect, it means you are loved and

forgiven. It means God heard your cries and He's bottled up, and thrown away every single worry. God desires that you live a good and graceful life, forgetting those things in your past. He wants you obedient, He wants you to know you're worthy of being happy and that you will find peace and contentment in Him. He wants you to always know that He's just a prayer away, that His door is always open to you.

Being gracefully broken means that no matter what battle you're facing, today or tomorrow that God is always here for you, He's your constant help.

Prayer: Father, help me with my over-thinking. Help me to lay all the things that trouble me at your feet. I

receive that I'm gracefully broken. I know you had to break me in order to humble me. Help me to continue to study the word of God so that I can apply it to my life and so I'm able to see and recognize your work in me. As I grow through the transition of being broken gracefully; allow me to recognize your favor over me and over everyone attached to me. Have your way in my life Lord, I surrender totally to you.
~Amen

Day 15

Prayer Changes Things

Psalm 15:29 KJV The Lord is far from the wicked, but he hears the prayer of the righteous.

Prayer changes things is more than just a cliche' saying. God hears our prayers and He desires that we pray unto Him regarding the issues and situations we face daily. Coming before Him first; with repentance and thanksgiving. When we pray we must believe by faith, that God will give us the desires of our hearts.. Praying and requesting things should never be the only reason we pray. We

should make it a constant habit of coming to The Lord with prayers of thanksgiving for the things He's already done. We must remember also, God blesses us, according to His good and perfect will. Everything you want, doesn't necessarily mean that God will give it to you. The word of God tells us that His thoughts and His ways are unlike ours.

Prayer: Father, I pray that you will move me to pray on a daily basis, to pray about the things that trouble me. To pray to you with a heart of thanksgiving for the things that are to come. I bless your Holy name for being God my father, my helper, my healer and my comforter. In your son, Jesus' name. ~Amen

Day 16

He Gives Us Beauty For Ashes

Isaiah 61:3 NIV To bestow on them a crown of beauty instead of ashes, the oil of joy instead of mourning, and a garment of praise instead of a spirit of despair.

God is a gracious, kind, consistent and loving savior. He never holds us captive to our sin after repentance. The world and people in it will constantly remind you of what you did wrong, and how distasteful it was but God. Yet, He remembers our sin no more. The Lord gives us beauty for ashes, when we've

experienced brokenness in the past or we feel abused and worn. God doesn't hold us in the spirit of despair; He instead loves all over us, while we heal from the guilt and pains of our past. God loves us so much. It is God's desire for you to be completely whole in Jesus. God sent His son into the world not to condemn us, but that the world might be saved through Him. God's gift to us of beauty for ashes just shows us how much He really cares for us and our well-being.

Prayer: Thank you Heavenly Father for your love towards me. Thank you that because of the repentance of my sins I feel whole. Father, thank you for allowing me to not be in bondage. Thank you that I'm forgiven and set free to begin to plow, seed and nourish the

spiritual garden that you are beginning to grow up in me. ~Amen

Day 17

You Are The Salt Of The Earth

Matthew 5:16. Let your light so shine
before men, that they may see your good
works, and glorify your Father which is
in heaven.

The Lord desires that we be Christ-like,
he desires that we live a life free from sin
and destruction so that those who are lost

will see a noticeable difference in our lives. Walking in continual obedience and operating in the spirit of love isn't always easy, because people will try you and test you. God says stand your ground, remain unmovable, even in the

midst of chaos. Show others through your loving kindness what it looks like to be forgiving when wronged. Go that extra mile for your coworker or your neighbor even when it seems they're not grateful. Remember always that God said He would bless us abundantly for our good works. I take great happiness in knowing that I've pleased God by showing the lost, the hurt and unforgiven; just what it looks like to operate in the fruit of the spirit. It brings me joy to be pleasing in the site of God. Go out today and choose to do something spectacular and amazing for someone who doesn't know Christ.

Prayer: Lord Jesus, I come to you seeking direction. Help me to be the daughter with whom you are well

pleased. Help me to easily forgive when hurt and wronged. Help me to pray earnestly for my enemies and for those who pretend to be my friends for their own gain. Keep me prayerful and willing to forgive others just as you have forgiven me. Allow me Father to exercise good works, so that others would inquire about you. Allow me Father, to be the salt and savor of the earth so that many will see me lead by example, therefore causing other unbelievers to realize that glorifying our Father in heaven is not only a gift but will allow them to recognize there is exceeding joy in serving you. ~Amen

Day 18

Peace And Joy

Phillippians 4:6-7 NIV Be anxious for nothing; but in every thing by prayer and supplication with thanksgiving let your requests be made known unto God. And the peace of God, which passeth all understanding, shall keep your hearts and minds through Christ Jesus.

Are you dealing with depression and or fear? Do you have negative thoughts and tend to expect things to end in a dreadful, hurtful way? Perhaps you feel that the weight of the world is on your shoulders, you're having problems thinking clearly

because bad always seems to be present in your life and situations. Sis, God promised you joy. We're told in the Word of God to rejoice always. The peace of God is powerful enough to guard you against those negative attacks that the enemy tries to bring to you. The enemy wants to stunt your spiritual growth. He desires to keep you bound and unhappy. Jesus can give you peace, one way to ensure that you walk and operate in the peace of God is to stay in constant prayer. You will experience the

joy and promises when you bring your
cares and concerns unto Him. He's
concerned about all things concerning
you. God will give you His joy in
abundance when you lay your concerns
and worries at His feet. God is a

comforter. He will make all things well
on your behalf.

Prayer: Father, I pray that you will
continue to bless me. In those times
when I allow negative thoughts and
worry to consume me, push me to pray. I
trust your will and your way. I also know
that I'm nothing without you. Teach me
your ways, help me to understand and
trust that you are always here for me; all

I have to do is call on you in my time of
need. ~ Amen

Day 19

Watch What You Say

Proverbs 16:24 Pleasant words are as an
honeycomb, sweet to the soul, and health
to the bones.

What are you talking about? Hopefully,
you are talking about things that are
positive. I pray you are encouraging

others by speaking love and life over them. So many times in life, we say whatever we want. We neglect to think about how someone may perceive what we're delivering. The scripture tells us to use words in our conversations that are pleasant and sweet as a honeycomb. Speaking words that are sweet to the

soul. If you've been speaking unpleasant things or talking foul to others rudely; today is the perfect day to make a conscious decision to change the way you are speaking to others. As believers we can be great examples of what it looks like to love others unconditionally. When we choose to speak kind, loving words to them, they'll see a difference and most will see love. Today's a great day to start speaking kind words, God will be well pleased.

Prayer: Heavenly Father, I need your help in speaking words to others that are kind. I want to be your daughter who pleases you with my works. I ask you to continue to press upon my heart and change my heart posture. Allow me to not be easily offended by the things that others do or say to me. Move me to pray for others daily. And in my speaking to others keep me focused on doing those things that are loving and kind so that I can be seen as showing good servantship to them. Prevent me from being rude and angry instead allow me to spread the love of Jesus as I communicate. ~Amen

Day 20

Sisterhood

Psalm 133:1 Behold, how good and how
pleasant it is for brethren to dwell
together in unity.

My sister, though we aren't biological;
We are related in the Spirit, oh how I

love thee. We pray together, lunch together and you are my sister, my friend, my godly- confidant. You show me what peace looks like. You exemplify what joy feels like. You're my greatest encourager and you check me when I'm wrong. Thank you my god-sister for holding me accountable when I fail. You

continue to reiterate to me what the Word of God instructs us to do when I choose to lean to my own understanding. We dwell together in unity, but we also dwell together in spirit. Sis, you nurture me with your friendship, you support me in love and you keep me on the right track; therefore allowing me not to fail. With you in my life and the gift of sisterhood I'm able to cultivate the art of trusting and accepting that we can all dwell together peacefully.

Prayer: Thank you Father for my god-sister. I thank you for her love, guidance and her acceptance. When I feel all alone, hurt and fearful; my sister is there to pray for me and bring me back

to reality. She reminds me Father, that you said I'm fearfully and wonderfully made. She encourages me to seek you when I'm clueless in my decisions. Thank you Lord for my forever friend; who is willing to keep pointing me toward the direction of righteousness and who will pray with and for me at any hour. I Thank you Jesus for her. ~Amen

Day 21

Anger Management

James 1:19 KJV , my beloved brethren,
let every man be swift to hear, slow to
speak, slow to wrath.

How we handle our anger speaks loudly
to the one who is attempting to offend us.
Our Heavenly Father tells us to be quick
to hear others, yet; to be slow to speak
and even slower to anger. If we take the
time to truly listen to others; we may hear
their pain, we may see their confusion
and we just might be able to minister to
them. Think about it. If we keep a
positive attitude, the hurting

individuals might look at us and inquire
as to why we're so joyful or where and
what is our source of peace. Losing our
cool or our temper simply because
someone was rude doesn't help or
produce anything other than continued
strife. As believers we must practice
what we preach. When offended, it's
vitally important not to react. Ask God at

that very moment to fill you with His
love and patience and to give you the
words to say. In doing so, you are slowly
working on your own anger management.

Prayer: Father I pray that you would help
me to control my anger when offended
and attacked. Help me to be the daughter
you have called me to be, I will lead by
example in the mighty name of Jesus!
Help me to realize at that very moment

that the greatest response is either silence
or a kind word, allowing me to realize
that my Christlike example of how I
handle offenses is what matters most. At
that very moment Lord, remove any
frustration from me, so that I can be
pleasing in your sight and in the sight of
those who offend me that they may see

your glory all over me in the Precious
Name of Jesus. ~Amen

Day 22

Peacemakers

Matthew 5:9 KJV Blessed are the
peacemakers: for they shall be called the
children of God.

Walking in and practicing the art of this beatitude isn't always easy but Jesus when he gave the Sermon On The Mount, He knew what He wanted to say to the disciples. Jesus wants believers to act according to the law. Money nor position of authority was of no interest to Him. Jesus taught what He expected; He expects obedience from the heart. Every beatitude came from Jesus from the heart of Jesus. He wants us to take all of them

as a source of "Code of Ethics" for believers. So, the peacemakers are blessed and shall be called children of God. In order to be a peacemaker; Sis, you've got to be at peace first and foremost. A peacemaker can act as a mediator; they can be a go-between for someone who may have gone silent after experiencing an unpleasant bout of communication with another person. Peacemakers help others to resolve conflict, they bring harmony to situations that might otherwise be filled with strife. Peacemakers are atmosphere changers, their goal is to help others to achieve their successes peacefully. Ask yourself, am I Jesus' example of a peacemaker? If not, what can I do to change that?

Prayer: Lord, I desire to honor your laws of The Beatitudes. I desire to be a peacemaker, I desire to be an atmosphere changer specializing in peace. Father, make me whole. Fix, mend and change anything that is unlike you. Remove any stronghold that would prevent me from walking in my peaceful purpose. Allow

me to grow spiritually where I can be
used not only to honor you; But through
you, allow me to be able to help those
who may have lost their voice. This
prayer I graciously submit unto you in
Jesus name. ~Amen

Day 23

Point Of Contact

Psalms 34:4 KJV I sought the LORD,
and he heard me, and delivered me from
all my fears.

Today allow The Lord to be your point of contact. Just as when you are new to a job or even a new location you don't know which way to go. There is always a site map and there is your point of contact. As your point of contact; The Lord can give you specific directions on how to handle situations. He is our point of contact regarding all things. He tells us that when we need things to ask and

we shall receive. Our point of contact gives us direction on which way to go; when to speak and even when to be quiet. Our point of contact even shares with us how we need to act in faith, how we are to have faith the grain of a mustard seed to usher things into fruition. He's our manager when we don't know how we should do things. We are taught through prayer, fasting and studying the Word of God; He leads us on the right path to success. God, our point of contact is all knowing; He's Alpha & Omega the beginning and the end. He's the perfect point of contact because He knows things far before we even acknowledge a need for what we think we need. Trust Him today to be your ultimate point of contact for all things in and for your life.

Prayer: Heavenly Father, allow me to realize you are The Original Source. You are my point of contact in all things. Nothing is too hard for you. When my faith waivers, when my direction is cloudy, lead me directly to you. When I can get help from nowhere let me go to The One & Only true living God who is

able to guide, renew and keep me on the
path of your righteousness. ~Amen

Day 24

Godly Wisdom

Proverbs 4:7 KJV Wisdom is the
principal; therefore get wisdom: and with
all thy getting get an understanding.

Webster's dictionary has more than one meaning of the word; wisdom. I'm going to use the definition that applies to this devotional. The definition of "wisdom" is one who has a wise attitude. To be wise is to be knowledgeable; A person with wisdom possesses the attribute of being intelligent. There are godly benefits that come with having godly wisdom. Some of the benefits are, We're promised a long and prosperous life. We obtained

favor with God and with other people. God will protect us, and we will therefore, walk peacefully. Wisdom is a gift we can ask God for and He said, "He'd freely give it". What will you do with your gift of wisdom?

Prayer: Father, bless me with the gift of wisdom. I need wisdom for all things. What I should and shouldn't partake in.

How or where I should go. Jesus, give me the wisdom that I can freely use to help others, also that I can use to give you all the glory and honor for my God-given gift. ~Amen

Day 25

Everything Belongs To God

Psalms 24:1-2 The earth is the LORD's and everything in it, the world, and all who live in it; 2 for he founded it upon

the seas and established it upon the
waters.

The LORD has graciously blessed us
with all that we have. We are to be good
stewarts and or caretakers of the earth.
We are to be thankful for this world as
well as the resources provided to us while
in it. However, the LORD never
intended for us, to get so caught up in the
world nor the things of this world

because this world will surely pass away
according to scripture. The Lord owns it
all, and everything within it. You are

blessed with your possessions not
because of the work you've done to
obtain them; But because of the creative,
wonderful and gracious God who blessed
you with the gift to even take part in His

creation. Thank God today. Seriously,
think about it, had there been no creation
of heaven nor earth. There would be no
you. Christ owns it all.

Prayer: Lord, we thank you. For every
single thing you've given us in your
beautiful creation of earth. You created
me. I thank you. I thank you for giving
man the wisdom, so that we can have the

things we need. Lord, you left nothing
out. Everything we need you've
provided. Thank you for all you do and
all you have done in my life. ~Amen

Day 26

No Weapon Formed Against You

Isaiah 54:17 KJV

No weapon that is formed against thee shall prosper; and every tongue that shall rise against thee in judgment thou shalt condemn. This is the heritage of the servants of the Lord, and their righteousness is of me, saith the Lord.

When the world and your enemies speak ill against you, and should they try to attack you; God says they shall be condemned. Tribulation and troubles may come. But the LORD said they will not

prosper. The Lord is our protector, He goes before us and He will keep you. In the midst of affliction you shall not be burned. God will be your help and He will ensure that you are not consumed by the attacks of your enemy. Trust The Lord to cover and protect you.

Prayer: Heavenly Father Thank you for your constant hedge of protection. Thank you Father for never leaving me, for not allowing hurt nor harm to come near me or mine. I am so grateful that you hold back many attacks, those I've never seen. You said no weapon formed against shall prosper I trust you LORD to silence the verbal attacks and continue to keep me encouraged even when I'm faced with

trials and tribulation. I thank you Oh God for continuing to protect and keep in the realm of your righteous hand. In Jesus' wonderful name I pray. ~Amen.

Day 27

Marital Disagreements

1 Corinthians 16:14 NIV Do everything in love.

God calls us as believers to do everything in love. He ordained marriage, therefore the husband and wife are to act in love even when we are angry. When disagreements arise; someone has to be the person who suggests prayer. Nothing good will come out of you both being angry. Marital bliss is work, but everything good is worth the work. Praying together constantly and talking things out will ensure marital bliss.

Oftentimes in a marriage, one or the other assumes too much. The key to marital bliss isn't who's right or wrong. The key is loving one another enough to seek Godly marital counseling should the issue be too big for you two to handle alone. Forgiveness is a huge factor as well. Choose to forgive one another and move forward. It's important that you realize that your love for one another is much more important than the actual reason you had the disagreement. Work together to mend the broken pieces and trust God to be at the forefront of your union.

Prayer: Heavenly Father forgive me when I fail. Please help me and my husband to love one another more and to be able to

communicate more effectively. Remove all the anger and resentment from me,

LORD. Bless and cover my husband. Renew our love for one another. Give us better communication. Allow us to trust you in our marriage. When disagreements arise and LORD I know they will; help both he and I to know that you, Father are our constant help in our

marriage and in our lives. We thank you
Jesus for all you've afforded us and all
we do. ~Amen

Day 28

God Has Plans For You

Jeremiah 29:11 NIV For I know the
thoughts that I think toward you, and
those are thoughts of good and not of
evil, but to bring you to an expected end.

God loves you. He created you. Even before you became a believer, God knew you. He knows all about you. He's also very concerned about all things concerning you. His thoughts toward you have always been good, yet God allows you to make your decisions. Be encouraged in your life, when things seem to be going in the direction you didn't expect, cry out to God; Seek Him for guidance. He will help. He's always here for us, we walk away from Him. So, if you're struggling with things, God can assist. Ask Him to help you with the things you are having a rough time dealing with. He will help you, but you must be obedient. There will be some good days and there will be some bad ones. Just remember He knows what He desires for you. Pray and ask God what is His will for your life. He has great plans for you.

Prayer: Father, I thank you for everything. Thank you for what you've blessed me with thus far. I want to be the daughter you have called me to be. Help me to make wise decisions as it's my desire to be pleasing in your sight. I need you to intervene, I need your divine direction. I have made horrible decisions

and I want to do better in my decision making process. I know that you love me. I love you too and I know your leading me is the very best for me; as you make no mistakes. In Jesus name, ~Amen

Day 29

Love One Another

John 15:12 KJV This is my
commandment, That ye love one another,
as I have loved you.

The LORD desires that we keep His
commandments. We are to live a life of
obedience. Obedience in the eyesight of
God is being kind, treating others the way
we desire to be treated. We are not to be
vindictive nor are we to be envious of
others and the things they have. God
wants us to work together, in love. We
are to pray for one another and do well to
all mankind. He wants us to love one

another. It's so much easier to love and
treat others well than it is to hate.

Prayer: Father help me to love others as
you love me. Help me to show love in
my actions, and in absolutely everything
I do. Allow the love I share to draw
others to Christ. ~Amen

Day 30

Proverbs 31:30 KJV Favour is deceitful, and beauty is vain: but a woman that feareth the LORD, she shall be praised.

To fear and love the LORD wholeheartedly in all that we do is beautiful. He is our Father and we are his daughters, we are descendants of royalty.

It's so wonderful to be in a relationship with such an awesome God, the One And Only true living God. He doesn't desire that we waste valuable time trying to please and get the approval of others. God is more concerned with our love for mankind. What are we doing as a servant ? Are we using our time to be loving, giving and forgiving? God desires that we show what it truly looks like to be an obedient, loving Daughter of A King.

Prayer: Lord Jesus fill me up with your love. Allow me to be a daughter that brings your heart joy. Please help me to not be distracted with the things of this world that don't matter. I'd like to work to receive the rewards you've promised by my living and walking in the LOVE of Christ. Thank you Jesus. ~Amen

Day 31

TRIUMPH !

Romans 8:28 All things work together for the good of those who love the LORD, who have been called according to His purpose.

Triumph means great victory or achievement. We achieve greatly when we surrender our lives totally over to Jesus Christ. He helps us to TRIUMPH through what can be seen as difficult circumstances. Surrender doesn't mean we won't have adversity but it does mean that The LORD will walk with us and we'll never feel alone. There truly is victory in Jesus. Victory in Jesus is triumph….Sis, you're WINNING! In Jesus we have life and when He died for us at Calvary; Jesus showed us one of the

greatest acts of love ever. Jesus could have quickly put an end to all the pain and ridicule suffered. However, he chose to take the pain. Christ in fact died at The Cross so that you could choose to live a life of TRIUMPH. No matter what's going on; with Jesus Christ in your life you will always TRIUMPH!

Prayer: Father, thank you for the gift of eternal life. Thank you that by my giving my life over to you and the repentance of my sins, I now have the promise of eternal life. Having you Father in my life and as head of my life is the ULTIMATE in TRIUMPH in itself. Thank you for the cleansing of my sins and for making me over again; Now, that's true TRIUMPH! Bless your Holy Name for the great and mighty things you have done and continue to do in my life in YOUR son's JESUS' name, I graciously pray. ~Amen

Closing Words: To every reader, this devotional was written with you and love in mind. I pray that God will use the words I've shared in this devotional to lead you to Christ, to encourage and strengthen you. I truly love you all with the love of Christ. ♥☐

I am Carol, a Daughter of Zion. An ordained minister, I'm a wife to Will, my OMAZING husband. A mother, a grand-mommy , a sister, a friend and now an author of my first book and I give glory and honor to God for His many blessings bestowed upon my life. I'm

truly grateful for every God-given
opportunity. Blessings unto you all.

Made in the USA
Monee, IL
14 November 2023

46525127R00057